to

_____

from

_____

date

_____

Ellie Claire® Gift & Paper Expressions
Franklin, TN 37067
EllieClaire.com
Ellie Claire is a registered trademark of Worthy Media, Inc.

Shine On Journal
© 2016 by Ellie Claire
Published by Ellie Claire, an imprint of Worthy Publishing Group,
a division of Worthy Media, Inc.

ISBN 978-1-63326-145-7

Stock or custom editions of Ellie Claire titles may be purchased in bulk for
educational, business, ministry, fundraising, or sales promotional use. For
information, please e-mail info@EllieClaire.com

Art © Shutterstock | shutterstock.com

Printed in China

1 2 3 4 5 6 7 8 9 – 21 20 19 18 17 16

Shine On

DEVOTIONAL

Ellie Claire®
gift & paper expressions

Contents

For the LORD your God is living among you.
He is a mighty savior.
He will take delight in you with gladness.
With his love, he will calm all your fears.
He will rejoice over you with joyful songs.

ZEPHANIAH 3:17 NLT

$\mathcal{Y}$ou are a beautiful woman of God, precious to Him in every way. As you seek Him, He will show you the mysteries of life and share His unique plans for you—a life full of rich blessing.

God cares about you and knows all the desires of your heart. He is as close as breathing. May this gift book encourage you to embrace your dreams and shine on.

Be strong in the Lord, and may His light guide your heart always.

The Most
Beautiful Things

May God give you
eyes to see beauty
only the heart
can understand.

Taking joy in life is a woman's best cosmetic.

ROSALIND RUSSELL

The best and most beautiful
things in the world cannot
be seen or even touched.
They must be felt with the heart.

HELEN KELLER

You are God's created beauty
and the focus of His affection and delight.

JANET WEAVER SMITH

Isn't it a wonderful morning? The world looks like something God had just imagined for His own pleasure.

Lucy Maud Montgomery

As God's workmanship, we deserve to be treated, and to treat ourselves, with affection and affirmation, regardless of our appearance or performance.

Mary Ann Mayo

Just as each day brims with your beauty, my mouth brims with praise.

Psalm 71:8 msg

In all ranks of life the human heart yearns for the beautiful, and the beautiful things that God makes are His gift to all alike.

Harriet Beecher Stowe

God has a wonderful plan for each person....
He knew even before He created this world
what beauty He would bring forth from our lives.

LOUISE B. WYLY

One cannot collect all the beautiful shells
on the beach. One can collect only a few,
and they are more beautiful if they are few.

ANNE MORROW LINDBERGH

A strong positive mental attitude
will create more miracles than any wonder drug.

PATRICIA NEAL

I've never seen a smiling face that was not beautiful.

*Y*our beauty and love chase after me
every day of my life.
I'm back home in the house of God
for the rest of my life.

PSALM 23:6 MSG

Beauty puts a face on God.
When we gaze at nature,
at a loved one, at a work of art,
our soul immediately
recognizes and is drawn to the face of God.

MARGARET BROWNLEY

$\mathcal{Y}$ou should clothe yourselves...with the beauty
that comes from within, the unfading beauty of a gentle
and quiet spirit, which is so precious to God.

1 Peter 3:4 nlt

Beauty without virtue is a flower without perfume.

Something deep in all of us
yearns for God's beauty,
and we can find it no matter where we are.

Sue Monk Kidd

$\mathcal{L}$et there be many windows in your soul,
That all the glory of the universe may beautify it.

Ella Wheeler Wilcox

$\mathcal{G}$od who is goodness and truth is also beauty.
It is this innate human and divine longing,
found in the company of goodness and truth,
that is able to recognize and leap up at beauty
and rejoice and know that all is beautiful,
that there is not one speck of beauty under the sun
that does not mirror back the beauty of God.

Roberta Bondi

*It is an extraordinary and beautiful thing that God,
in creation...works with the beauty of matter;
the reality of things; the discoveries of the senses,
all five of them; so that we, in turn, may hear
the grass growing; see a face springing to life
in love and laughter.... The offerings of creation...
our glimpses of truth.*

Madeleine L'Engle

Blessings Are Extraordinary Gifts

Some blessings like rainbows
after rain or a friend's
listening ear are extraordinary gifts
waiting to be discovered
in an ordinary day.

Strength, rest, guidance, grace,
help, sympathy, love—
all from God to us! What a list of blessings!

EVELYN STENBOCK

Lift up your eyes. Your heavenly Father waits
to bless you—in inconceivable ways to make
your life what you never dreamed it could be.

ANNE ORTLUND

All the way my Saviour leads me—
What have I to ask beside?
Can I doubt His tender mercy,
Who through life has been my guide?
Heavenly peace, divinest comfort,
Here by faith in Him to dwell!
For I know, what'er befall me,
Jesus doeth all things well.

FANNY J. CROSBY

When You grant a blessing,
O LORD, it is an eternal blessing!

1 Chronicles 17:27 nlt

I will let God's peace infuse every
part of today. As the chaos swirls
and life's demands pull at me on all sides,
I will breathe in God's peace that surpasses
all understanding. He has promised
that He would set within me a peace
too deeply planted to be affected
by unexpected or exhausting demands.

Let God's promises shine on your problems.

Corrie ten Boom

*M*ay your footsteps set you upon
a lifetime of love.
May you wake each day
with His blessings and sleep
each night in His keeping,
and may you always walk
in His tender care.

*Add to your joy
by counting your blessings.*

*God has not promised sun without rain,
joy without sorrow, peace without pain.
But God has promised strength for the day,
rest for the labor, light for the way,
grace for the trials, help from above,
unfailing sympathy, undying love.*

ANNIE JOHNSON FLINT

$\mathcal{B}$lessed is the person who is too busy to worry in the
daytime and too sleepy to worry at night.

CAROLINE SCHROEDER

I wish I had a box,
the biggest I could find,
I'd fill it right up to the brim
with everything that's kind.
A box without a lock, of course,
and never any key;
for everything inside that box
would then be offered free.
Grateful words for joys received
I'd freely give away.
Oh, let us open wide a box
of praise for every day.

$\mathcal{H}$ow great is your goodness,
which you have stored up for those who fear you,
which you bestow in the sight of men
on those who take refuge in you.

PSALM 31:19 NIV

Tarry at the promise till God meets you there.
He always returns by way of His promises.

L. B. COWMAN

I will bless you; I will make your name great,
and you will be a blessing.

GENESIS 12:2

We don't have to be perfect to be a blessing.
We are asked only to be real, trusting in His perfection
to cover our imperfection, knowing that one day we will
finally be all that Christ saved us for and wants us to be.

GIGI GRAHAM TCHIVIDJIAN

*L*ive your life while you have it.
Life is a splendid gift—there is nothing small about it.

FLORENCE NIGHTINGALE

I am convinced beyond a shadow of any doubt that the most valuable pursuit we can embark upon is to know God.

KAY ARTHUR

*G*ive generously, save consistently,
and never spend more money than you have.

MARY HUNT

At the end of your life you will never regret not having passed one more test, not winning one more verdict, or not closing one more deal. You will regret time not spent with a husband, a friend, a child, or a parent.

BARBARA BUSH

Sweet Contentment

Love, consolation, and peace bloom only in the garden of sweet contentment.

MARTHA ANDERSON

Women of adventure have conquered their fates
and know how to live exciting and fulfilling lives right
where they are. They have learned to reinvent themselves
and find creative ways to enjoy the world and their
place in it. They know how to take mini-vacations,
stop and smell the roses, and live fully in the moment.

BARBARA JENKINS

*Contentment is not the fulfillment of what you want,
but the realization of how much you already have.*

You're blessed when you're content
with just who you are—no more, no less.
That's the moment you find yourselves proud
owners of everything that can't be bought.

MATTHEW 5:5 MSG

*It is always wise to stop
wishing for things long enough
to enjoy the fragrance
of those now flowering.*

PATRICE GIFFORD

*An unhurried sense of time
is in itself a form of wealth.*

BONNIE FRIEDMAN

Where the soul is full of peace and joy,
outward surroundings and circumstances
are of comparatively little account.

HANNAH WHITALL SMITH

If you're content to simply be yourself,
your life will count for plenty.

MATTHEW 23:11 MSG

Let the day suffice, with all its joys and failings,
its little triumphs and defeats. I'd happily,
if sleepily, welcome evening as a time of rest,
and let it slip away, losing nothing.

KATHLEEN NORRIS

I am still determined to be cheerful and happy,
in whatever situation I may be;
for I have also learned from experience
that the greater part of our happiness
or misery depends upon our dispositions,
and not upon our circumstances.

MARTHA WASHINGTON

Our fulfillment comes in knowing God's glory, loving Him for it, and delighting in it.

*For I have learned to be content whatever
the circumstances. I know what it is to be in need,
and I know what it is to have plenty. I have learned
the secret of being content in any and every situation,
whether well fed or hungry,
whether living in plenty or in want.*

PHILIPPIANS 4:11–12

Life is not intended to be simply a round of work,
no matter how interesting and important
that work may be. A moment's pause to watch
the glory of a sunrise or a sunset is soul satisfying,
while a bird's song will set the steps to music all day long.

LAURA INGALLS WILDER

Normal day, let me be aware of
the treasure you are. Let me learn from you,
love you, bless you before you depart.
Let me not pass you by in quest
of some rare and perfect tomorrow.

*The splendor of the rose and the whiteness
of the lily do not rob the little violet of its scent
nor the daisy of its simple charm. If every tiny flower
wanted to be a rose, spring would lose its loveliness.*

THÉRÈSE OF LISIEUX

To love is to be content with
the present moment, open to its meaning,
entering into its mystery.

ELIZABETH O'CONNOR

*Happy times and bygone days are never lost....
In truth, they grow more wonderful
within the heart that keeps them.*

KAY ANDREW

The thought of You stirs us so deeply that we cannot be content unless we praise You, because You have made us for Yourself and our hearts find no peace until they rest in You.

AUGUSTINE

Let the message about Christ,
in all its richness, fill your lives....
Sing psalms and hymns
and spiritual songs to God
with thankful hearts.

COLOSSIANS 3:16 NLT

Sing songs to the tune of his glory,
set glory to the rhythms of his praise.

PSALM 66:2 MSG

Encouragement for Your Heart

The Scriptures give us hope
and encouragement as we wait
patiently for God's promises
to be fulfilled.

ROMANS 15:4 NLT

God created us with an overwhelming
desire to soar. Our desire to develop and use
every ounce of potential He's placed in us
is not egotistical. He designed us to be
tremendously productive and "to mount up
with wings like eagles," realistically dreaming
of what He can do with our potential.

CAROL KENT

God makes our lives a medley of joy and tears,
hope and help, love and encouragement.

I wanted you to see what real courage is....
It's when you know you're licked before
you begin but you begin anyway
and you see it through no matter what.

HARPER LEE

Moments spent listening, talking, playing,
and sharing together may be the most important times of all.

GLORIA GAITHER

Hope begins in the dark, the stubborn hope
that if you just show up and try to do
the right thing, the dawn will come.
You wait and watch and work: you don't give up.

ANNE LAMOTT

For we have great joy and consolation in your love,
because the hearts of the saints have been refreshed by you.

PHILEMON 1:7 NKJV

So when some dear joy loses
its beauteous summer glow,
Think how the roots of roses
are kept alive in the snow.

ALICE CARY

When we take time to notice the simple things
in life, we never lack for encouragement.
We discover we are surrounded by a limitless hope
that's just wearing everyday clothes.

*M*ay our Lord Jesus Christ himself
and God our Father encourage you
and strengthen you in every good thing you do and say.

2 Thessalonians 2:16 ncv

*Every day we live is a priceless gift of God,
loaded with possibilities to learn
something new, to gain fresh insights.*

Dale Evans Rogers

*E*ncouragement is being a good listener,
being positive, letting others know
you accept them for who they are.
It is offering hope, caring about
the feelings of another, understanding.

Gigi Graham Tchividjian

*We are so preciously loved by God that we cannot
even comprehend it. No created being can ever know
how much and how sweetly and tenderly God loves them.*

Julian of Norwich

$\mathcal{A}$ word of encouragement to those we meet,
a cheerful smile in the supermarket,
a card or letter to a friend, a readiness
to witness when opportunity is given—
all are practical ways in which
we may let His light shine through us.

ELIZABETH B. JONES

There are times when
encouragement means such a lot
And a word is enough to convey it.

GRACE STRICKER DAWSON

$\mathcal{C}$alm me, O Lord, as You stilled the storm,
Still me, O Lord, keep me from harm.
Let all the tumult within me cease,
Enfold me, Lord, in Your peace.

CELTIC TRADITIONAL

Some days, it is enough encouragement
just to watch the clouds break up and disappear,
leaving behind a blue patch of sky
and bright sunshine that is so warm upon my face.
It's a glimpse of divinity; a kiss from heaven.

*The stars exist
that we might know how high
our dreams can soar.*

*Everyone has inside himself a piece of good news!
The good news is that you really don't know
how great you can be, how much you can love,
what you can accomplish and what your potential is.*

ANNE FRANK

The Scriptures give us hope and encouragement
as we wait patiently for God's promises to be fulfilled.

ROMANS 15:4 NLT

Hope floods my heart with delight!
Running on air, mad with life, dizzy, reeling,
Upward I mount—faith is sight, life is feeling....
I am immortal! I know it! I feel it!

MARGARET WITTER FULLER

But joyful are those who have the God of Israel
as their helper, whose hope is in the LORD their God.

PSALM 146:5 NLT

Be strong and let your heart take courage,
all you who hope in the LORD.

PSALM 31:24 NASB

A Treasury of Faith

In the end, I think this
is what women truly desire:
to know God and to stand tall
in their faith, strong at the core,
tender in heart.

RUTH SENTER

Faith means being sure of what we hope for...now.
It means knowing something is real, this moment,
all around you, even when you don't see it.
Great faith isn't the ability to believe long and far
into the misty future. It's simply taking
God at His word and taking the next step.

JONI EARECKSON TADA

Now faith is the substance of things hoped for,
the evidence of things not seen.

HEBREWS 11:1 NKJV

The soft, sweet summer was warm and glowing,
Bright were the blossoms on every bough:
I trusted Him when the roses were blooming;
I trust Him now....

L. B. COWMAN

*Y*ou are a child of your heavenly Father.
Confide in Him. Your faith in His love
and power can never be bold enough.

BASILEA SCHLINK

Only she who can see the invisible can do the impossible.

*T*he LORD your God is indeed God.
He is the faithful God who keeps his covenant
for a thousand generations and lavishes
his unfailing love on those who love
him and obey his commands.

DEUTERONOMY 7:9 NLT

*Faith sees the invisible, believes the incredible,
and receives the impossible.*

I believe in the sun even if it isn't shining.
I believe in love even when I am alone.
I believe in God even when He is silent.

Faith is the first factor in a life devoted to service.
Without faith, nothing is possible.
With it, nothing is impossible.

MARY MCLEOD BETHUNE

If it can be verified, we don't need faith....
Faith is for that which lies on the other side of reason.
Faith is what makes life bearable, with all its tragedies
and ambiguities and sudden, startling joys.

MADELEINE L'ENGLE

Faith expects from God what is beyond all expectations.

Within each of us there is an inner place where the living
God Himself longs to dwell, our sacred center of belief.

There is no unbelief;
Whoever plants a seed beneath the sod
And waits to see it push away the clod,
She trusts in God.

ELIZABETH YORK CASE

Faith is not an effort, a striving, a ceaseless seeking,
as so many earnest souls suppose, but rather a letting go,
an abandonment, an abiding rest in God that nothing,
not even the soul's shortcomings, can disturb.

I think miracles exist in part as gifts
and in part as clues that there is something
beyond the flat world we see.

PEGGY NOONAN

I took an inventory and looked into my little bag to see
what I had left over. I had one jewel left in the bag,
the brightest jewel of all. I had the gift of faith.

LOLA FALANA

*L*et love and faithfulness never leave you;
bind them around your neck,
write them on the tablet of your heart.

PROVERBS 3:3

*Faith has to be exercised in the midst of ordinary,
down-to-earth living.*

ELISABETH ELLIOT

I see heaven's glories shine,
And faith shines equal, arming me from fear.

EMILY BRONTË

*There is an activity of the spirit, silent, unseen, which must
be the dynamic of any form of truly creative, fruitful trust.
When we commit a predicament, a possibility, a person to God
in genuine confidence, we do not merely step aside and tap
our foot until God comes through. We remain involved.
We remain in contact with God in gratitude and praise.
But we do this without anxiety, without worry.*

EUGENIA PRICE

I love the L ORD because he hears my voice
and my prayer for mercy. Because he bends down to listen,
I will pray as long as I have breath!

P SALM 116:1–2 NLT

Intimacy may not be rushed....
We can't dash into God's presence
and choke down spiritual inwardness
before we hurry to our one o'clock appointment.

C ALVIN M ILLER

$\mathcal{B}$ ehold, I stand at the door and knock.

R EVELATION 3:20 NASB

God waits to give to those who ask Him
a wisdom that will bind us to Himself,
a wisdom that will find expression
in a spirit of faith and a life of faithfulness.

J. I. P ACKER

The Love of Family

Family faces are magic mirrors.
Looking at people who belong to us,
we see the past, present, and future.

GAIL LUMET BUCKLEY

$\mathcal{H}$ome. A place where when you get there,
you know your heart has been there all along.

GLORIA GAITHER

*Sooner or later we all discover that the important
moments in life are not the advertised ones,
not the birthdays, the graduations, the weddings,
not the great goals achieved. The real milestones are
less prepossessing. They come to the door of memory.*

SUSAN B. ANTHONY

$\mathcal{P}$lease, bless my family.
Let it continue before you always.
Lord GOD, you have said so.

2 SAMUEL 7:29 NCV

*I feel from a spiritual standpoint
that there's a real celebration of humanity,
of the common bond of everybody.
We need each other.*

AMY GRANT

We really need only five things on this earth:
some food, some sun, some work,
some fun, and someone.

BEATRICE NOLAN

Love allows us to live,
and through living
we grow in loving.

EVELYN MANDEL

The effect of having other interests beyond
those domestic works well. The more one does
and sees and feels, the more one is able to do,
and the more genuine may be one's appreciation
of fundamental things like home, and love,
and understanding companionship.

AMELIA EARHART

$\mathcal{A}$s if that weren't enough, you've blessed
my family so that it will continue
in your presence always.
Because you have blessed it, GOD,
it's *really* blessed—blessed for good!

1 CHRONICLES 17:27 MSG

We were a strange little band of characters,
trudging through life sharing diseases and toothpaste,
coveting one another's desserts, hiding shampoo,
borrowing money, locking each other out of our rooms,
inflicting pain and kissing to heal it in the same instant,
loving, laughing, defending, and trying to figure out
the common thread that bound us all together.

ERMA BOMBECK

$\mathcal{F}$amilies give us many things—love and meaning,
purpose and an opportunity to give, and a sense of humor.

When you look at your life, the greatest happinesses are family happinesses.

JOYCE BROTHERS

We are so very rich if we know just a few people in a way in which we know no others.

CATHERINE BRAMWELL-BOOTH

*What families have in common the world around
is that they are the place where people
learn who they are and how to be that way.*

JEAN ILLSLEY CLARKE

Finally, all of you should be in agreement, understanding each other, loving each other as family, being kind and humble.

1 PETER 3:8 NCV

Our job is not to straighten each other out,
but to help each other up.

NEVA COYLE

More and more I realize that everybody, regardless of age,
needs to be hugged and comforted in a brotherly
or sisterly way now and then. Preferably now.

JANE HOWARD

Family is of the utmost importance to me. But my family
is no more perfect than [any other].... We love, trust, get
hurt, sometimes outraged, and we love and trust anyhow,
because that's the best way to let our love grow.

MADELEINE L'ENGLE

The greatest gift we can give one another is
rapt attention to one another's existence.

SUE ATCHLEY EBAUGH

If we are cheerful and contented, all nature smiles...
the flowers are more fragrant, the birds sing
more sweetly, and the sun, moon, and stars all appear
more beautiful, and seem to rejoice with us.

ORISON SWETT MARDEN

Rejoice! Celebrate all the good things that GOD,
your God, has given you and your family.

DEUTERONOMY 26:10–11 MSG

That's His song, the one He's been singing:
I rejoice in you. Come rejoice in Me. This is song that
plays the world to life, that follows everywhere I go,
song that fuels joy: Enjoy Me. Enjoy Me!

ANN VOSKAMP

You have chosen to bless my family....
LORD, you have blessed my family,
so it will always be blessed.

1 CHRONICLES 17:27 NCV

Nothing Like a True Friend

Insomuch as any one
pushes you nearer to God,
he or she is your friend.

FRENCH PROVERB

I cannot count the number of times I have been
strengthened by another woman's heartfelt hug,
appreciative note, surprise gift, or caring questions....
My friends are an oasis to me, encouraging me to go on.
They are essential to my well-being.

DEE BRESTIN

Knowing what to say is not always necessary;
just the presence of a caring friend
can make a world of difference.

SHERI CURRY

What shall I bestow upon a friend?
Gay laughter to sustain when sorrow
may bring pain, a bright song of life,
a belief that winter ends in the glory of spring,
and a prayer of hope for peace that will forever stay.

LEA PALMER

$\mathcal{A}$ friend understands what you are trying to say...
even when your thoughts aren't fitting into words.

ANN D. PARRISH

Rich is the woman
who has a praying friend.

JANICE HUGHES

$\mathcal{F}$riendship is the fruit gathered from
the trees planted in the rich soil of love,
and nurtured with tender care and understanding.

ALMA L. WEIXELBAUM

Perfume and incense bring joy to the heart,
and the pleasantness of a friend
springs from their heartfelt advice.

PROVERBS 27:9

The happiest business in all the world
is that of making friends,
And no investment on the street
pays larger dividends,
For life is more than stocks and bonds,
and love than rate percent,
And she who gives in friendship's name
shall reap what she has spent.
Thank you for the treasure of your friendship...
for showing me God's special heart of love.

A friend hears the song in my heart
and sings it to me when my memory fails.

Reliable friends who do what they say
are like cool drinks in sweltering heat—refreshing!

PROVERBS 25:13 MSG

60

*If we would build on a sure foundation
in friendship, we must love friends
for their sake rather than for our own.*

CHARLOTTE BRONTË

Uhen you are truly joined in spirit,
another woman's good is your good too.
Your work for the good of each other.

RUTH SENTER

*Don't walk in front of me—I may not follow.
Don't walk behind me—I may not lead.
Walk beside me—and just be my friend.*

There are some friends you know you will have
for the rest of your life. You're welded together by love,
trust, respect, or loss—or simple embarrassment.

We should all have one person who knows
how to bless us despite the evidence.

PHYLLIS THEROUX

*I am only as strong as the coffee I drink,
the hairspray I use, and the friends I have.*

This is My commandment, that you love one other
as I have loved you. Greater love has no one than this,
than to lay down one's life for his friends.

JOHN 15:12–13 NKJV

*A true friend is one who is concerned about what
we are becoming, who sees beyond the present relationship and
cares deeply about us as a whole person.*

GLORIA GAITHER

*H*aving someone who understands
is a great blessing for ourselves. Being someone
who understands is a great blessing to others.

JANETTE OKE

Gratitude unlocks the fullness of life.
It turns what we have into enough,
and more.... It can turn a meal into a feast,
a house into a home, a stranger into a friend.
Gratitude makes sense of our past,
brings peace for today,
and creates a vision for tomorrow.

MELODY BEATTIE

True gratitude, like true love,
must find expression
in acts, not words.

R. MILDRED BARKER

You Have a Gift

There's a special kind of freedom
women enjoy: freedom to share
innermost thoughts, to ask a favor,
to show their true feelings.
The freedom simply to be themselves.

$\mathcal{A}$s women, we want to know we are important
and that we have a significant place in our world.
We need to know that we matter to someone,
that our lives are making a difference in the lives
of other people, that we are able to touch their souls.
This desire to have value is God-given.

BEVERLY LAHAYE

*If your lips can speak a word
of encouragement to a weary soul,
you have a talent.*

EVA J. CUMMINGS

$\mathcal{E}$ach one of us is God's special work of art.
Through us, He teaches and inspires,
delights and encourages,
informs and uplifts all those who view our lives.

JONI EARECKSON TADA

I have filled him with the Spirit of God, with skill, ability and knowledge in all kinds of crafts.

EXODUS 31:3

When I stand before God at the end of my life,
I would hope that I would not have a single bit of talent left
and could say, "I used everything You gave me."

ERMA BOMBECK

This is the real gift: you have been given
the breath of life, designed with a unique,
one-of-a-kind soul that exists forever—
the way that you choose to live
it doesn't change the fact that you've
been given the gift of being now and forever.
Priceless in value, you are handcrafted by God,
who has a personal design and plan for each of us.

$\mathcal{N}$o one can arrive from being talented alone.
God gives talent, work transforms talent into genius.

ANNA PAVLOVA

*We all have different gifts, each of which came because
of the grace God gave us.... Anyone who has the gift
of serving should serve. Anyone who has the gift of teaching
should teach. Whoever has the gift of encouraging others
should encourage. Whoever has the gift of giving to others
should give freely. Anyone who has the gift of being a leader
should try hard when he leads. Whoever has the gift
of showing mercy to others should do so with joy.*

ROMANS 12:6–8 NCV

$\mathcal{G}$od does not ask your ability or your inability.
He asks only your availability.

MARY KAY ASH

*E*very one has a gift for something,
even if it is the gift of being a good friend.

MARIAN ANDERSON

*Since you are like no other being
ever created since the beginning of time,
you are incomparable.*

BRENDA UELAND

*G*od gave me my gifts. I will do all I can
to show Him how grateful I am to Him.

GRACE LIVINGSTON HILL

*Giving encouragement to others is a most welcome gift,
for the results of it are lifted spirits,
increased self-worth, and a hopeful future.*

FLORENCE LITTAUER

*L*ord...give me the gift of faith to be renewed
and shared with others each day.
Teach me to live this moment only,
looking neither to the past with regret,
nor the future with apprehension.
Let love be my aim and my life a prayer.

ROSEANN ALEXANDER-ISHAM

God's designs regarding you,
and His methods of bringing about
these designs, are infinitely wise.

MADAME JEANNE GUYON

*I*t is clear to us, friends, that God not only
loves you very much but also has put
His hand on you for something special.

1 THESSALONIANS 1:4 MSG

*Your life is a gift from God, and it is a privilege
to share it. Today and always, know that you have
a very special place in others' hearts—and in His.*

$\mathcal{E}$verything in life is most fundamentally a gift.
And you receive it best, and you live it best,
by holding it with very open hands.

LEO O'DONOVAN

People should eat and drink and enjoy the fruits of their labor,
for these are gifts from God.

ECCLESIASTES 3:13 NLT

Time is a very precious gift of God;
so precious that it's only given to us moment by moment.

AMELIA BARR

The free gift of God is eternal life
through Christ Jesus our Lord.

ROMANS 6:23 NLT

Is there a greater way to love the Giver
than to wildly delight in His gifts?

ANN VOSKAMP

God Our Father

I need not lack now any more
For any lovely thing;
I need to know my birthright for
My Father is the King!

EVELYN GAGE

Tuck [this] thought into your heart today.
Treasure it. Your Father God cares about
your daily everythings that concern you.

KAY ARTHUR

Whoever walks toward God one step,
God runs toward him two.

JEWISH PROVERB

God is every moment totally aware of each one of us.
Totally aware in intense concentration and love....
No one passes through any area of life, happy or tragic,
without the attention of God.

EUGENIA PRICE

As a rose fills a room with its fragrance,
so will God's love fill our lives.

MARGARET BROWNLEY

We continually recall before God our Father the things you have done because of your faith and the work you have done because of your love.

1 Thessalonians 1:3 ncv

Before anything else, above all else, beyond everything else, God loves us. God loves us extravagantly, ridiculously, without limit or condition. God is in love with us...God yearns for us.

Roberta Bondi

God is the sunshine that warms us, the rain that melts the frost and waters the young plants. The presence of God is a climate of strong and bracing love, always there.

Joan Arnold

The treasure our heart searches for is found in the ocean of God's love.

Janet Weaver Smith

$\mathcal{N}$othing we can do will make the Father love us less;
nothing we do can make Him love us more.
He loves us unconditionally with an everlasting love.
All He asks of us is that we respond
to Him with the free will that He has given to us.

NANCIE CARMICHAEL

God is the Father who is full of mercy
and all comfort. He comforts us every time
we have trouble, so when others have trouble,
we can comfort them with the same comfort God gives us.

2 CORINTHIANS 1:3-4 NCV

$\mathcal{T}$he Creator thinks enough of you to have sent
Someone very special so that you might have life—
abundantly, joyfully, completely, and victoriously.

God will never let you be shaken or moved from your place near His heart.

JONI EARECKSON TADA

We do not need to search for heaven, over here or over there, in order to find our eternal Father. In fact, we do not even need to speak out loud, for though we speak in the smallest whisper or the most fleeting thought, He is close enough to hear us.

TERESA OF AVILA

The God who created, names, and numbers the stars in the heavens also numbers the hairs of my head.... He pays attention to very big things and to very small ones. What matters to me matters to Him, and that changes my life.

ELISABETH ELLIOT

People who don't know God and the way he works fuss over these things, but you know both God and how he works. Steep yourself in God-reality, God-initiative, God-provisions. You'll find all your everyday human concerns will be met.

MATTHEW 6:32–33 MSG

*Don't be afraid of missing out.
You're My dearest friends! The Father
wants to give you the very kingdom itself.*

LUKE 12:30–32 MSG

Stand outside this evening. Look at the stars. Know that you are special and loved by the One who created them. You have the joy of this assurance— the heavenly Father will always answer prayer, and He knows—just how much you can bear.

PHYLLIS HALL

$\mathcal{E}$ven when all we see are the tangled threads
on the backside of life's tapestry, we know that
God is good and is out to do us good always.

RICHARD J. FOSTER

*No eye has seen, no ear has heard, and no mind has imagined
what God has prepared for those who love him.*

1 CORINTHIANS 2:9 NLT

This life is not all. It is an "unfinished symphony"...
with those who know that they are related to God
and have felt the power of an endless life.

HENRY WARD BEECHER

*For God is, indeed, a wonderful Father who longs
to pour out His mercy upon us, and whose majesty
is so great that He can transform us from deep within.*

TERESA OF AVILA

A Heart Full of Gratitude

Happiness is a healthy
mental attitude,
a grateful spirit,
a clear heart full of love.

If it is God who gives prayer, then God often gives
it in the form of gratitude, and gratitude itself,
when it is received attentively in prayer,
is healing to the heart. Prayer is such a mysterious
business for something so ordinary and everyday.

ROBERTA BONDI

That I am here is a wonderful mystery
to which I will respond with joy.

Enter into His gates with thanksgiving,
and into His courts with praise.
Be thankful to Him, and bless His name.

PSALM 100:4 NKJV

$\mathcal{M}$ost of the people I know who have what I want—
which is to say, purpose, heart, balance, gratitude, joy—
are people with a deep sense of spirituality....
They are part of something beautiful.

ANNE LAMOTT

Appreciation is like salt—a little goes
a long way to bring out the best in us.

$\mathcal{G}$ratitude unlocks the fullness of life.
It turns what we have into enough, and more....
It can turn a meal into a feast, a house into a home,
a stranger into a friend. Gratitude makes sense
of our past, brings peace for today,
and creates a vision for tomorrow.

MELODY BEATTIE

True gratitude, like true love,
must find expression in acts, not words.

R. MILDRED BARKER

Were there no God we would be in this glorious
world with grateful hearts and no one to thank.

CHRISTINA ROSSETTI

Feeling grateful or appreciative of someone or something
in your life actually attracts more of the things that you
appreciate and value into your life. And, the more of your
life that you like and appreciate, the healthier you'll be.

CHRISTIANE NORTHRUP

Give thanks to the LORD, for he is good!
His faithful love endures forever.

1 CHRONICLES 16:34 NLT

I am convinced that God has built into all of us
an appreciation of beauty and has even allowed us
to participate in the creation of beautiful things
and places. It may be one way God brings healing
to our brokenness, and a way that we can contribute
toward bringing wholeness to our fallen world.

MARY JANE WORDEN

To receive a gift, molded from love and sacrifice,
selected with care and tied up with all the excitement
the giver has to offer, is indeed rare. They don't
come along often, but when they do, cherish them.

ERMA BOMBECK

Give thanks to God. Call out his name.
Ask him anything! Shout to the nations, tell them
what he's done, spread the news of his great reputation!

ISAIAH 12:4 MSG

Let us begin from this moment
to acknowledge Him in all our ways,
and do everything, whatsoever we do,
as service to Him and for His glory,
depending upon Him alone for wisdom,
and strength, and sweetness, and patience.

HANNAH WHITALL SMITH

Being grateful for what we have today doesn't mean we
have to have that forever. It means we acknowledge that
what we have today is what we're supposed to have today.
There is enough.... And all we need will come to us.

MELODY BEATTIE

Enter His gates with thanksgiving
And His courts with praise.
Give thanks to Him, bless His name.

PSALM 100:4 NASB

Gratitude consists in a watchful, minute attention to the particulars of our state, and to the multitude of God's gifts, taken one by one. It fills us with a consciousness that God loves and cares for us, even to the least event and smallest need of life.

HENRY EDWARD MANNING

True gratitude, like true love,
must find expression in acts, not words.

R. MILDRED BARKER

Shine On

It doesn't take
a huge spotlight
to draw attention
to how great our God is.
All it takes is for
one committed person
to...let his light shine.

GARY SMALLEY AND JOHN TRENT

89

$\mathcal{M}$ay you be filled with joy, always thanking the Father.
He has enabled you to share in the inheritance
that belongs to his people, who live in the light.
For he has rescued us from the kingdom of darkness.

COLOSSIANS 1:11–13 NLT

God shall be my hope, my stay,
my guide and lantern to my feet.

WILLIAM SHAKESPEARE

I pray that your hearts will be flooded with light
so that you can understand the confident hope he
has given to those he called—his holy people
who are his rich and glorious inheritance.

EPHESIANS 1:18 NLT

Light shines on the godly,
and joy on those whose hearts are right.
May all who are godly rejoice in the LORD
and praise his holy name!

PSALM 97:11–12 NLT

Dear Lord...shine through me, and be so in me
that every soul I come in contact with may feel
Your presence in my soul.... Let me thus praise You
in the way You love best, by shining on those around me.

JOHN HENRY NEWMAN

Just as a prism of glass miters light and casts
a colored braid, a garden sings sweet incantations
the human heart strains to hear. Hiding in every flower,
in every leaf, in every twig and bough, are reflections
of the God who once walked with us in Eden.

TONIA TRIEBWASSER

All that is desirable in things is an image
of the supremely desirable God.... There is simply nothing
else to desire except God or God's images and reflections....
All the different things we desire are really one;
for they are reflections of aspects of God.

PETER KREEFT

Our feelings do not affect God's facts. They may blow up, like clouds, and cover the eternal things that we do most truly believe. We may not see the shining of the promises— but they still shine! [His strength] is not for one moment less because of our human weakness.

AMY CARMICHAEL

God infuses...joy from the surprises of life, which unexpectedly brighten our days, and fill our eyes with light.

SAMUEL LONGFELLOW

$\mathcal{B}$y reading of Scripture I am so renewed that all nature seems renewed around me and with me. The sky seems to be a purer, a cooler blue, the trees a deeper green, light is sharper on the outlines of the forest, and the hills and the whole world is charged with the glory of God.

THOMAS MERTON

When we give the Word of God space
to live in our heart, the Spirit of God
will use it to take root,
penetrating the earthiest recesses of our lives.

KEN GIRE

$\mathcal{S}$end me your light and your faithful care,
let them lead me; let them bring me
to your holy mountain, to the place
where you dwell. Then I will go to the
altar of God, to God, my joy and my delight.
I will praise you with the lyre, O God, my God.

PSALM 43:3–4

*It is the LORD who provides the sun to light the day
and the moon and stars to light the night,
and who stirs the sea into roaring waves.*

JEREMIAH 31:35 NLT

Finding Joy

All who seek the LORD
will praise him. Their hearts will
rejoice with everlasting joy.

PSALM 22:26 NLT

Taking joy in life is a woman's best cosmetic.

ROSALIND RUSSELL

How necessary it is to cultivate a spirit of joy.
It is a psychological truth that the physical acts
of reverence and devotion make one feel devout.
The courteous gesture increases one's respect for others.
To act lovingly is to begin to feel loving,
and certainly to act joyfully brings joy to others
which in turn makes one feel joyful.
I believe we are called to the duty of delight.

DOROTHY DAY

I pray that the God who gives hope
will fill you with much joy and peace
while you trust in him. Then your hope
will overflow by the power of the Holy Spirit.

ROMANS 15:13 NCV

To be able to find joy in another's joy,
that is the secret
of happiness.
Where does constant joy abound?
In the restless social round,
Entertainment in excess,
Worldly charm or cleverness?
Fleeting are their seeming gains.
Joy is found where Jesus reigns.

HALLIE SMITH BIXBY

As we grow in our capacities to see and enjoy the joys that God has placed in our lives, life becomes a glorious experience of discovering His endless wonders.

God makes our lives a medley of joy and tears, hope and help, love and encouragement.

Our hearts were made for joy. Our hearts were made to enjoy the One who created them. Too deeply planted to be much affected by the ups and downs of life, this joy is a knowing and a being known by our Creator. He sets our hearts alight with radiant joy.

A joyful heart is like a sunshine of God's love,
the hope of eternal happiness, a burning flame of God....
And if we pray, we will become that sunshine of God's love—
in our own home, the place where we live,
and in the world at large.

MOTHER TERESA

Happiness comes of the capacity to feel deeply, to enjoy simply, to think freely, to risk life, to be needed.

STORM JAMESON

When hands reach out in friendship,
hearts are touched with joy.

If one is joyful, it means that one is faithfully living
for God, and that nothing else counts;
and if one gives joy to others one is doing God's work.

With joy without and joy within, all is well.

JANET ERSKINE STUART

You have to look for the joy. Look for the light of God
that is hitting your life, and you will find
sparkles you didn't know were there.

BARBARA JOHNSON

Happiness is something that comes into our lives through
doors we don't even remember leaving open.

ROSE WILDER LANE

Remember: Each of us can
decrease the suffering of the world
by adding to its joy.

DAWNA MARKOVA

The LORD is my strength and my shield;
my heart trusts in him, and I am helped.
My heart leaps for joy
and I will give thanks to him in song.

PSALM 28:7

Be truly glad. There is wonderful joy ahead....
You love him even though you have never seen him.
Though you do not see him now, you trust him;
and you rejoice with a glorious, inexpressible joy.

1 PETER 1:6, 8 NLT

With God, life is eternal—both in quality and length. There is no joy comparable to the joy of discovering something new from God, about God. If the continuing life is a life of joy, we will go on discovering, learning.

EUGENIA PRICE

Those the LORD has rescued will return.
They will enter Zion with singing; everlasting joy
will crown their heads. Gladness and joy
will overtake them, and sorrow and sighing will flee away.

ISAIAH 35:10

In Your presence is fullness of joy;
At Your right hand are pleasures forevermore.

PSALM 16:11 NKJV

Herein is joy, amid the ebb and flow
of the passing world: our God remains unmoved,
and His throne endures forever.

ROBERT COLEMAN

Laughter Is Good for the Soul

Take time to laugh.
It is the music of the soul.

What a circus we women perform every day of our lives.
It puts a trapeze artist to shame.

ANNE MORROW LINDBERGH

Our mouths were filled with laughter,
our tongues with songs of joy.

PSALM 126:2

Laughing at ourselves as well as with each other
gives a surprising sense of togetherness.

HAZEL C. LEE

Confidence is the feeling you have
before you understand the situation.

The best laughter, the laughter that can heal,
the laughter that has the truest ring, is the laughter
that flowers out of a love for life and its Giver.

MAXINE HANCOCK

*This is a test. It is only a test. If this were your actual life,
you would be given better instructions.*

MYRNA NEIMS

If you don't have wrinkles, you haven't laughed enough.

PHYLLIS DILLER

*Whole-hearted, ready laughter heals, encourages,
relaxes anyone within hearing distance. The laughter
that springs from love makes wide the space around—
gives room for the loved one to enter in.*

EUGENIA PRICE

You can't turn back the clock.
But you can wind it up again.

BONNIE PRUDEN

A cheerful look brings joy to the heart;
good news makes for good health.

PROVERBS 15:30 NLT

Sense of humor; God's great gift
causes spirits to uplift,
Helps to make our bodies mend;
lightens burdens; cheers a friend;
Tickles children; elders grin
at this warmth that glows within;
Surely in the great hereafter
heaven must be full of laughter!

Experience is something you don't get
until just after you need it.

$\mathcal{P}$eople can be divided into three groups:
Those who make things happen,
those who watch things happen,
and those who wonder what happened.

*A good laugh is as good
as a prayer sometimes.*

LUCY MAUD MONTGOMERY

Today's Forecast: Partly rational
with brief periods of coherent thought
giving way to complete apathy by tonight.

SHERRIE WEAVER

*Can it be an accident that "stressed"
is "desserts" spelled backwards?*

SUSAN MITCHELL

Anxiety weighs down the heart,
but a kind word cheers it up.

PROVERBS 12:25

"I wonder why people say 'Amen' and not 'A women'?"
Bobby questioned. His little friend replied,
"Because they sing hymns and not hers, silly."

Blessed are they who can laugh at themselves,
for they shall never cease to be amused.

If you can learn to laugh in spite of the circumstances
that surround you, you will enrich others,
enrich yourself, and more than that, you will last!

BARBARA JOHNSON

$\mathcal{M}$y soul will rejoice in the LORD
and delight in his salvation.

PSALM 35:9

Joy is more than my spontaneous expression
of laughter, gaiety, and lightness. It is deeper
than an emotional expression of happiness.
Joy is a growing, evolving manifestation of God
in my life as I walk with Him.

BONNIE MONSON

$\mathcal{H}e$ made you so you could
share in His creation, could love
and laugh and know Him.

TED GRIFFEN

111

Love All Around

Open your hearts to the love
God instills.... God loves you
tenderly. What He gives you
is not to be kept under
lock and key, but to be shared.

MOTHER TERESA

113

*L*ove is extravagant in the price it is willing to pay,
the time it is willing to give,
the hardships it is willing to endure,
and the strength it is willing to spend.

JONI EARECKSON TADA

*Let's practice real love. This is the only way
we'll know we're living truly, living in God's reality.
It's also the way to shut down debilitating self-criticism....
For God is greater than our worried hearts
and knows more about us than we do ourselves.
And friends, once that's taken care of
and we're no longer accusing or condemning ourselves,
we're bold and free before God!*

1 JOHN 3:18–21 MSG

*Among God's best gifts to us
are the people who love us.*

There is no need to plead that the love of God shall
fill our hearts as though He were unwilling to fill us....
Love is pressing around us on all sides like air.
Cease to resist it and instantly love takes possession.

AMY CARMICHAEL

*Oh, if we did but love others! How easily the least thing,
the shutting of a door gently, the walking softly,
speaking low, not making a noise, or the choice of a seat,
so as to leave the most convenient to others,
might become occasions of its exercise.*

MÈRE ANGÉLIQUE ARNAULD

*L*ove...bears all things,
believes all things,
hopes all things,
endures all things.
Love never fails.

1 Corinthians 13:4, 7–8 nkjv

Only He who created the wonders of the world entwines hearts in an eternal way.

Trying to find yourself within yourself is like peeling the layers off an onion. When you finish you have nothing but a pile of peelings. The only way to find yourself is to go outside of yourself and love another.

Rhonda S. Hogan

What we have once enjoyed we can never lose.
All that we love deeply becomes a part of us.

HELEN KELLER

Let us love so well
our work shall still be sweeter for our love,
and still our love
be sweeter for our work.

ELIZABETH BARRETT BROWNING

Love grows from our capacity
to give what is deepest within ourselves
and also receive what is the deepest within
another person. The heart becomes an ocean
strong and deep, launching all on its tide.

You gave me life and showed me your unfailing love.
My life was preserved by your care.

JOB 10:12 NLT

*Nothing can separate you from His love,
absolutely nothing.... God is enough for time,
and God is enough for eternity. God is enough!*

HANNAH WHITALL SMITH

Today, see if you can stretch your heart
and expand your love so that it touches
not only those to whom you can give it easily,
but also those who need it so much.

DAPHNE ROSE KINGMA

There is no fear in love; but perfect love casts out fear, because fear involves punishment, and the one who fears is not perfected in love.

1 John 4:18 nasb

God is constantly taking knowledge of me in love, and watching over me for my good.

J. I. Packer

God has not given us a spirit of fear,
but of power and of love and of a sound mind.

2 Timothy 1:7 nkjv

Give Thanks and Sing Praise

Let us give all that lies within us...
to pure praise, to pure loving
adoration, and to worship from
a grateful heart a heart that
is trained to look up.

AMY CARMICHAEL

I will give thanks to the LORD because of his righteousness
I will sing praise to the name of the Lord Most High.

PSALM 7:17

Being grateful for what we have today doesn't mean we have to have that forever. It means we acknowledge that what we have today is what we're supposed to have today. There is enough.... And all we need will come to us.

Thanksgiving puts power in living,
because it opens the generators of the heart
to respond gratefully, to receive joyfully,
and to react creatively.

Thank You, God, for little things
That often come our way,
The things we take for granted
But don't mention when we pray.
The unexpected courtesy,
The thoughtful kindly deed,
A hand reached out to help us
In the time of sudden need.
Oh, make us more aware, dear God,
Of little daily graces
That come to us with sweet surprise
From never-dreamed-of places.

Let's praise His name! He is holy, He is almighty.
He is love. He brings hope, forgiveness, heart cleansing,
peace, and power. He is our deliverer and coming King.
Praise His wonderful name!

LUCILLE M. LAW

I will thank you, Lord, among all the people.
I will sing your praises among the nations.

PSALM 57:9 NLT

Morning has broken like the first morning,
Blackbird has spoken like the first bird....
Praise with elation, praise every morning,
God's re-creation of the new day!

ELEANOR FARJEON

Let us always offer to God our sacrifice of praise,
coming from lips that speak his name.
Do not forget to do good to others,
and share with them, because such sacrifices please God.

HEBREWS 13:15–16 NCV

Live today fully, expressing gratitude
for all you have been,
all you are right now,
and all you are becoming.

MELODY BEATTIE

Our thanksgiving today should include
those things which we take for granted,
and we should continually praise our God,
who is true to His promise, who has provided
and retained the necessities for our living.

BETTY FUHRMAN

*L*ike supernatural effervescence, praise will sometimes
bubble up from the joy of simply knowing Christ.
Praise like that is...delight. Pure pleasure!
But praise can also be supernatural determination.
A decisive action. Praise like that is...quiet resolve.
Fixed devotion. Strength of spirit.

JONI EARECKSON TADA

*May your life become one of glad and unending praise
to the Lord as you journey through this world,
and in the world that is to come!*

TERESA OF AVILA

They that trust the Lord find many things
to praise Him for. Praise follows trust.

LILY MAY GOULD

I will always have hope;
I will praise you more and more.

Psalm 71:14

Praise is a place for God to be. A home place.
A workshop for His Holy Spirit in our lives.
It is an atmosphere of total openness where
He can be free to do good things in and through our days.

Gloria Gaither

How blessed are the people who know the joyful sound!
O Lord, they walk in the light of Your countenance.
In Your name they rejoice all the day,
And by Your righteousness they are exalted.

Psalm 89:15–16 nasb

Investing in Prayer

Allow your dreams a place in your
prayers and plans. God-given dreams
can help you move into the future
He is preparing for you.

BARBARA JOHNSON

129

We must take our troubles to the Lord,
but we must do more than that;
we must leave them there.

HANNAH WHITALL SMITH

What God gives in answer to our prayers
will always be the thing we most urgently need,
and it will always be sufficient.

ELISABETH ELLIOT

We need quiet time to examine
our lives openly and honestly....
Spending quiet time alone
gives your mind an opportunity
to renew itself and create order.

SUSAN L. TAYLOR

$\mathcal{B}$e kindly affectionate to one another...fervent in spirit,
serving the Lord; rejoicing in hope, patient in tribulation,
continuing steadfastly in prayer; distributing
to the needs of the saints, given to hospitality.

ROMANS 12:10–13 NKJV

There isn't a certain time
we should set aside to talk about God.
God is part of our every waking moment.

MARVA COLLINS

$\mathcal{O}$pen wide the windows of our spirits and fill
us full of light; open wide the door of our hearts
that we may receive and entertain Thee
with all the powers of our adoration.

CHRISTINA ROSSETTI

When we call on God, He bends down His ear to listen, as a father bends down to listen to his little child.

ELIZABETH CHARLES

Prayer is such an ordinary, everyday, mundane thing.
Certainly, people who pray are no more saints
than the rest of us. Rather, they are people
who want to share a life with God,
to love and be loved, to speak and to listen,
to work and to be at rest in the presence of God.

ROBERTA BONDI

If a care is too small to be turned into a prayer then it is too small to be made into a burden.

You pay God a compliment
by asking great things of Him

TERESA OF AVILA

The center of power is not to be found in summit meetings
or in peace conferences. It is not in Peking or Washington
or the United Nations, but rather where a child of God
prays in the power of the Spirit for God's will to be done
in her life, in her home, and in the world about her.

RUTH BELL GRAHAM

I thank my God every time I remember you.
In all my prayers for all of you, I always pray with joy.

PHILIPPIANS 1:3-4

It is when things go wrong, when good things
do not happen, when our prayers
seem to have been lost, that God is most present.

MADELEINE L'ENGLE

You will make your prayer to Him,
He will hear you.

Job 22:27 NKJV

Prayer is a long-term investment, one that will increase
your sense of security because God is your protector. Keep
at it every day, for prayer is the key of the day and the bolt
of the evening. God is waiting to hear from you.

BARBARA JOHNSON

It may seem strange to think that God wants
to spend time with us, but...think about it.
If God went to all the trouble to come to earth,
to live the life that He did, to die for us,
then there's got to be a hunger and a passion
behind that. We think of prayer as an "ought to,"
but in reality it is a response to God's
passionate love for us. We need to refocus
on the fact that God is waiting for us to show up and be
with Him and that our presence truly touches Him.

HENRY CLOUD

I know that God is faithful.
I know that He answers prayers,
many times in ways I may not understand.

SHEILA WALSH

Simplicity

It isn't the great big
pleasures that count
the most; it's making
a great deal out
of the little ones.

JEAN WEBSTER

𝒮ilences make the real conversations
between friends. Not the saying,
but the never needing to say is what counts.

Margaret Lee Runbeck

Happy people...enjoy the fundamental,
often very simple things of life....
They savor the moment, glad to be alive,
enjoying their work, their families,
the good things around them. They are adaptable;
they can bend with the wind, adjust to the changes
in their times, enjoy the contest of life....
Their eyes are turned outward; they are aware,
compassionate. They have the capacity to love.

Jane Canfield

In a world where it is necessary to succeed, perhaps...we women know more deeply that success can be a quiet and hidden thing.

PAM BROWN

Enjoy the little things.
One day you may look back
and realize...they were the big things.

So in everything, do to others
what you would have them do to you,
for this sums up the Law and the Prophets.

MATTHEW 7:12

While both boredom and serenity
address the passage of time,
the former yawns and rolls its eyes,
the latter sighs and revels in its value.

BARBARA FARMER

It's the little things that make up the richest part of the tapestry of our lives.

A fiery sunset, tiny pansies by the wayside,
the sound of raindrops tapping on the roof—
what extraordinary delight we find
in the simple wonders of life! With wide eyes
and full hearts, we may cherish what others often miss.

$\mathcal{A}$ devout life does bring wealth, but it's the rich simplicity
of being yourself before God. Since we entered the world
penniless and will leave it penniless, if we have bread
on the table and shoes on our feet, that's enough.

1 TIMOTHY 6:6 MSG

Not every day of our lives is overflowing with joy
and celebration. But there are moments
when our hearts nearly burst within us
for the sheer joy of being alive.
The first sight of our newborn babies,
the warmth of love in another's eyes,
the fresh scent of rain on a hot summer's eve—
moments like these renew in us
a heartfelt appreciation for life.

GWEN ELLIS

It is the simple things of life that make living worthwhile, the sweet fundamental things such as love and duty, work and rest, and living close to nature.

LAURA INGALLS WILDER

Don't ever let yourself get so busy that you
miss those little but important extras in life—
the beauty of a day...the smile of a friend...
the serenity of a quiet moment alone.
For it is often life's smallest pleasures and gentlest joys
that make the biggest and most lasting difference.

$\mathcal{M}$uch of what is sacred is hidden in the ordinary,
everyday moments of our lives. To see something
of the sacred in those moments takes slowing down
so we can live our lives more reflectively.

KEN GIRE

*I see nature...playing endless variations in design
and beauty.... In such simple yet eloquent ways,
I am reminded that God is personal,
revealing Himself continuously in the finite.*

JUDITH C. LECHMAN

$\mathcal{C}$ome and sit and ask Him whatever is on your heart.
No question is too small, no riddle too simple. He has all
the time in the world. Come and seek the will of God.

MAX LUCADO

You are a creation of God
unequaled anywhere in the universe.
God never made anyone else
exactly like you, and He never will again.
Thank Him for yourself and then
for all the rest of His glorious handiwork.

NORMAN VINCENT PEALE